STEAM ON BRITAIN'S MINIATURE RAILWAYS—$7\frac{1}{4}''$ to $15''$ gauge

RHYL
MINIATURE RLY.
BOOK HERE.
RHYL
TRAIN
RHYL

STEAM ON BRITAIN'S MINIATURE RAILWAYS

$7\frac{1}{4}''$ to $15''$ gauge

Robin Butterell

D. BRADFORD BARTON LIMITED

Frontispiece: Prince Edward of Wales, *a Bassett-Lowke Atlantic 4-4-2 'Little Giant', built in 1909 for the White City Exhibition as* Red Dragon, *leaves the station for a run on the 15in. gauge railway round the Marine Lake at Rhyl. Both the locomotive and the buildings in the background were the work of the famous miniature railway engineer, Henry Greenly. Bassett-Lowke were responsible for many of the early miniature locomotives either as standard types or built to special order. Their works at Northampton became world famous in later years for their small-scale working models of locomotives and ships. The firm still exists today but now only produces models to special order, mostly for demonstration purposes. This photograph is a copy of a sepia original in the offices of Rhyl Amusements and was taken in the early 1900s by a local photographer, Rae Pickard.*

ISBN 0 85153 237 3

Printed in Great Britain by H. E. Warne Ltd, London and St. Austell
for the publishers

D. BRADFORD BARTON LTD · Trethellan House · Truro · Cornwall · England

introduction

Passenger-carrying miniature railways have enjoyed a renaissance in Britain within the past twenty years. There seem to be a number of contributory reasons for this, but the chief one must be the desire to perpetuate fully operational steam locomotives, albeit in miniature form, after their disappearance from the national railway network.

A definition of the term miniature railway might be appropriate. The dividing line becomes somewhat tenuous in the larger gauges—was not the Festiniog Railway called the 'Toy Railway' in the 1930s?—but the best description seems to be that a miniature railway is one on which the locomotives, sometimes the rolling stock and occasionally the lineside accessories, are models of real or imaginary prototypes.

Miniature lines already in existence for many years, mostly of the larger gauge of 15in., have passed through difficult times but, like their narrow gauge compatriots, have entered a period of consolidation aided by fresh finance and enthusiastic volunteers. New lines have been built, in particular in the $7\frac{1}{4}$in. gauge, once the province of the rich private enthusiast who built such lines round his garden or estate for the amusement of himself and his friends, but now with ambitious locomotives based on narrow gauge prototypes providing the power and size of the early 15in. gauge designs. Inevitably, as will be seen from the illustrations that follow, chief interest is focussed on the locomotives. Rolling stock in the majority of cases and in particular in the smaller gauges is of simple and robust design to provide comfortable travel for overscale passengers who might find it difficult to shoehorn themselves into scale coaches. On the 15in. gauge one can be more ambitious as Sir Arthur Heywood, the pioneer in this work, showed, producing even restaurant and sleeping cars although the latter can hardly be taken seriously. The three most extensive lines in this gauge still in operation all have modern covered stock.

The first lines were built in the middle of the nineteenth century, but it was not until the early 1900s, when Bassett-Lowke the manufacturer joined with Greenly the engineer to produce the 'Little Giant' locomotives in 15in. gauge, that the miniature railway achieved any prominence in this country. By the 1920s and 1930s costs of labour and materials were rising and enthusiasts looked to the smaller gauges of $10\frac{1}{4}$in., $9\frac{1}{2}$in. and $7\frac{1}{4}$in. The latter is the smallest which can be laid at ground level and carry passengers in reasonable safety and comfort. The author has driven both 5in. and $3\frac{1}{2}$in. gauge locomotives at ground level and, while finding it an extremely exciting experience, the problem of the average human being's centre of gravity makes the whole business a somewhat hazardous operation.

The photographs in this volume, few of which have been previously published, chart the progress of the passenger-carrying miniature railway from 1905 to the present day. While it is impossible to include all the lines ever built, the cross-section shown may be said to be representative. The first part deals with the period before the first World War; this is followed by the 1920s and the 1930s, whilst the final section covers the period from the 1940s to the present day. In each of these divisions, public lines are followed by private; some of the latter are open to the public from time to time, but the author would enter a plea to respect their privacy as their public openings are generally well advertised.

Miniature meets narrow gauge on 15in. in 1905. The Class 10 4-4-2 Bassett-Lowke *Little Giant*, designed by Henry Greenly, being unloaded at Balderton station in Cheshire, where the Duke of Westminster's railway ran to Eaton Hall. The 0-6-0 *Shelagh*, designed by Sir Arthur Heywood, stands in the foreground. Work had started on *Little Giant* at Bassett-Lowke's work in Northampton in January and it was completed in 22 weeks. After the trials here it started work at Blackpool on Whit Monday. [Bassett-Lowke]

The 'Little Giant' reached its most advanced form in the first of the Class 30. *Synolda*, built for Sir Robert Walker, is here seen running on the line on his estate at Sand Hutton in Yorkshire soon after building in 1912. Impressed with the performance of this pleasure line, Sir Robert disposed of the 15in. gauge railway and constructed an 18in. gauge line to serve his estate. This change was due to the availability of suitable locomotives and rolling stock on the second-hand market.
[Bassett-Lowke]

J. E. P. Howey at Staughton Manor in Huntingdonshire in 1914 with his 4-6-2 *John Anthony*. This was basically a Class 30 'Little Giant' with an extra pair of driving wheels. Howey had already run a 9½in. gauge line with a Bassett-Lowke GN 4-4-2 Atlantic which was returned in part exchange for this 15in. gauge locomotive. Although only one example of this type was ever built, Bassett-Lowke showed it in their 1911 catalogue priced at £425! [Bassett-Lowke]

Cab view of a 'Little Giant', built in 1909. Note the simple but robust fittings. The locomotives had inside frames of ¼in. steel plates which were cut out by hand. Cylinders were 3¼in. × 6in. with 18in. diameter driving wheels while trailing and tender wheels were 11in. diameter. Boiler working pressure was 110lbs. p.s.i. weight of locomotive and tender 1 ton 12cwt. with bogie tender; cost was £345. [Bassett-Lowke]

W. J. BASSETT-LOWKE & Co.
MAKERS
NORTHAMPTON.
ENG-1909

J. T. Holder driving the $10\frac{1}{4}$in. gauge locomotive *John Terence* on his father's railway at Broome, near Stourbridge, in 1909. The bridge was specially built for the line at the Earl of Dudley's Ironworks.
[J. A. Holder]

NE 4-4-0 at Broome in 1909. This locomotive was converted to $9\frac{1}{2}$in. gauge by Grimshaw, Mr. Holder's engineer, for the 1925 Wembley Exhibition where it was renamed *Wendy*. After the exhibition closed, it was converted back to $10\frac{1}{4}$in. gauge, subsequently passing to the Farnborough Railway in 1938.
[J. A. Holder]

John Terence at Broome with J. T. Holder and his mother in 1909.
[J. A. Holder]

A 4-2-2 GN single wheeler on the turntable at Broome in 1910. The tender still bears the initials of the Pitmaston Moor Green Railway where it ran before coming to Broome. Subsequently it operated at Burnham-on-Sea in the 1930s.
[J. A. Holder]

Early four-wheel Bassett-Lowke rolling stock seating eight passengers for the 15in. gauge. This, and similar bogie vehicles, became standard for many lines, the awning being an optional extra. Some examples still exist today, a tribute to the quality of materials and workmanship some 60 years later. [Bassett-Lowke]

▷

0-8-2 *River Irt*, on the Ravenglass & Eskdale Railway in Cumbria, leaving the gauntletted track on the left as it brings a 15in. gauge train into Ravenglass in 1933. This was rebuilt from a Heywood locomotive, *Muriel*, in 1927. The standard gauge line, now removed, carried stone from the crushing plant at Murthwaite to the main line. [Mary Fair]

A four-cylinder Baltic locomotive designed by J. A. Holder in 1912. The chassis was built in Birmingham and the boiler by Goodhand. Parts of this locomotive were used by H. C. S. Bullock in the construction of a later locomotive *Audrey* and the inside cylinders were built into an 0-6-0 GW pannier tank which ran at Farnborough, New Romney and, finally, Hastings. [J. A. Holder]

River Mite on the Ravenglass & Eskdale at Dalegarth in 1933. This locomotive, a 4-6-0 + 0-6-4, was constructed from *Colossus*, a 4-6-2 originally owned by J. E. P. Howey and named *John Anthony*, together with another 4-6-2 built for the R & E by Hunt of Bournemouth, named *Sir Aubrey Brocklebank*. The hybrid was never a great success and was withdrawn in 1937. [Mary Fair]

Ravenglass station in 1933. A train pulls in headed by *River Esk*, a 2-8-2 designed by Henry Greenly and built by Davey Paxman in 1923. This locomotive was built to a scale of 4in. to the foot or one third full size, compared with *Colossus* and *Sir Aubrey Brocklebank*, which were models to one quarter full size, the more precise interpretation for the 15in. gauge. [Mary Fair]

River Esk and *River Irt* outside their shed at Ravenglass in 1934. Until the outbreak of the War in 1939 these two locomotives were responsible for the major part of steam-hauled traffic on the line.
[Mary Fair]

▷

A selection of tickets from the Ravenglass & Eskdale Railway, including some issued for special trains.

River Esk with a train at Ravenglass in 1928. In 1927 the locomotive was altered to form an articulated unit with the construction of a steam tender. Like the combination of the other two locomotives, this rebuild was not a success and in 1931 the tender reverted to a normal double-bogie vehicle; the frames and wheels thus made redundant were used as the basis of the new *River Mite*. [Mary Fair]

The original 15in. gauge railway at Blackpool, on which the locomotive *Little Giant* operated, was closed when the lease of the site ran out and a new layout was built on the outskirts of Halifax. This, again, was closed in due course and *Little Giant* was returned to Bassett-Lowke's Works at Northampton where it was completely overhauled and fitted with the bogie tender which had become standard for later locomotives of the class. It is shown here before being delivered in 1923 to its new owners at Sunny Vale, near Halifax, where it ran under the name of *Baby Bunce*. Later, it became the property of Tom Tate and is now running on his line at Haswell in County Durham. [Bassett-Lowke]

A scene on the 15in. gauge Fairbourne Railway near Barmouth on the West coast of Wales in August 1939. The locomotive is a Class 30 'Little Giant', *Count Louis*, constructed by Bassett-Lowke in Northampton for Count Louis Zborowski in 1923. After the latter was killed in 1924 it was purchased by the FR. The train consists of original Bassett-Lowke four-wheel stock, and is approaching Penrhyn Point, the terminus on the sand dunes opposite Barmouth. The three longer established and most important 15in. gauge railways in the country consist of the Fairbourne Railway, Romney Hythe & Dymchurch Railway and the Ravenglass & Eskdale Railway. [Robin Butterell]

Count Louis at Fairbourne terminus in August 1939. At this date the layout here consisted of a single run round loop with a corrugated iron shed for the storage of locomotives. Now a new terminus exists on the other side of the adjoining stream with covered accommodation for both locomotives and rolling stock. [Robin Butterell]

The Duke of York, later King George VI, stands by the *Northern Chief* on the Romney, Hythe & Dymchurch Railway on 5 August 1926. Construction of the 15in. railway had been pushed ahead so that the Duke could travel on the line at this time. As can be seen, only one track is complete.

[Collection: George Barlow]

Captain J. E. P. Howey, builder and owner of the RH & DR stands by No. 9, *Dr. Syn*, at the locomotive shed at New Romney soon after completion in 1931. This and the sister engine, No. 10, were built by the Yorkshire Engine Company from parts made at New Romney using boilers by Krauss of Munich.

[J. A. Holder]

Captain Howey in the cab of *Green Goddess* in May 1925 at Davey Paxman's works prior to the transportation of the locomotive to the Ravenglass & Eskdale Railway for trials. The Westinghouse brake was later removed and a vacuum brake added. Greenly's first design for the railway was based on Gresley's GN Pacifics. Davey Paxman had already built the one-third scale *River Esk* for the Ravenglass & Eskdale Railway and therefore they were a natural choice for the job. Unlike full size prototypes they had only two cylinders and were fitted with bogie tenders. It is possible for two people to sit side by side on the footplate although this restricts the driver's ability to shovel coal from behind his back to the firehole door. The weight in working order is just under 8 tons—an interesting comparison with *Little Giant*. [J. A. Holder]

The most ambitious $10\frac{1}{4}$in. gauge railway ever built ran from Farnborough Green to Camberley and was known as the Surrey Border & Camberley Railway. It was a continuation of the previous Farnborough Miniature Railway, being operated by Alexander Kinloch, a merchant banker. The locomotives, constructed by Bullock, were mostly of GW outline. The upper photograph shows a train leaving the main covered terminus and the lower a line-up of three Bullock locomotives, including a 2-6-0 + 0-6-2 Garratt, No. 4012, one of two built by Kitson for the line in 1938. [Collection: Robin Butterell]

By 1942, falling passenger traffic, due to the war, meant closure of the line and much of the equipment was sold or left lying derelict. Here, Bullock 4-6-2 *King Edward VIII*, in the boarded-up terminus, is surrounded by rolling stock and weeds. In the lower photograph, a derelict coach stands outside. The semi-scale rolling stock had lifting roof panels to facilitate entry. Although the locomotives and coaches were dispersed over a wide area, many are still operating on other railways today.

[Robin Butterell/ Gwyneth Schofield]

A $9\frac{1}{2}$in. gauge GN Atlantic built by Bassett-Lowke in the 1930s. It operated on a line at Harness Grove, near Worksop, owned by Captain Ward-Jones. Note the scale rolling stock. [Bassett-Lowke]

Another Bassett-Lowke $9\frac{1}{2}$in. gauge Atlantic—probably the most famous of them all. Originally bought by J. E. P. Howey for operation at Staughton Manor, the locomotive passed to J. A. Holder in 1925 and, named *Peter Pan*, ran on the Treasure Island Railway at Wembley Exhibition. As the railway was sponsored by the CPR, it was painted black with Canadian Pacific on the tender. J. T. Holder drove the locomotive when King George V and Queen Mary travelled on the train. After the Exhibition, the locomotive was converted to $10\frac{1}{4}$in. gauge by Grimshaw and went to Broome. In 1947 it was sold and eventually passed into private ownership after running for a short time at Bressingham. Below: *John Terence* on the Broome Railway in 1922, driven by an employee of Holder's Brewery.

[J. A. Holder]

In the early 1930s, the Broome Railway was moved to Holder's new house, called Keeping, in the New Forest, where *John Terence* makes an interesting contrast with J. A. Holder's SS Jaguar in 1936.
[J. A. Holder]

The Pacific *Audrey*, built by Bullock for the Keeping Railway in 1936, with J. A. Holder's 1903 6HP De Dion, now in the Montague Motor Museum.
[J. A. Holder]

This Baltic tank *Mary* was built by Bullock in 1932 for the Keeping Railway. Later a tender was added to provide space for coal and to augment the water supply.
[J. A. Holder]

The 'Walls Ice Cream Man' tries his hand at driving *Audrey* in 1937.
[J. A. Holder]

A freelance $9\frac{1}{2}$in. gauge Atlantic built by Parver Models of Southport in 1914. Rebuilt in 1962, it is shown on a line at the 'Kings Arms' public house, Cardington, in 1964. [Robin Butterell]

H. C. S. Bullock, the well-known builder of $10\frac{1}{4}$in. gauge locomotives, drives *John Terence* at Keeping in 1936. Note the train of scale coaches originally constructed for use in a film. [J. A. Holder]

Kerr's $10\frac{1}{4}$in. gauge miniature railway at Arbroath alongside the NE main line in 1948. On the right is a Bullock 4-6-2, *Silver Jubilee*. The locomotive on the left, although of steam outline, is driven by a petrol engine. [Matthew Kerr]

The Fairbourne Railway on Whit Monday 1951. John Wilkins, who had then recently acquired the line, stands behind the tender of *Count Louis*, which is little altered from pre-war days. The line had changed hands in 1946 when almost derelict and a great deal of work to both track and rolling stock was required before running started again.
[Robin Butterell]

Designed by Twining and built by Guest, 2-4-2 *Sian* at Fairbourne in the 1960s. A combination of GW and narrow gauge influence produced a handsome and efficient locomotive. Trevor Guest, who has been responsible for several $10\frac{1}{4}$in. and 15in. gauge locomotives designed by E. W. Twining, received through the post one day a superb perspective of a freelance engine. Twining said that this was the locomotive that he would like Guest to build. The result was *Katie*, a sister locomotive to *Sian* which was built especially for the Fairbourne Railway.
[Robin Butterell]

The 15in. gauge Dreamland Miniature Railway at Margate in the 1950s. In the background is a Greenly-designed 4-4-2 built by Barnes of Rhyl in 1928. Greenly felt that the 'Little Giant' required enlarging to increase power and this was the result. *Prince Edward of Wales* in the foreground is a 'Little Giant' built by Bassett-Lowke in 1909, starting life at the Franco-British Exhibition at the White City, Shepherd's Bush and named *Red Dragon*. [Robin Butterell]

Having lain derelict for some years at Margate, *Prince Edward of Wales* was purchased privately and is shown here having been transported to Hampshire prior to overhaul. It is now the property of the author and W. H. McAlpine together with another 'Little Giant', *George the Fifth*. Both locomotives are being rebuilt by Roger Marsh at Hinckley. [Robin Butterell]

A rare photograph of all four Barnes Atlantics standing outside the locomotive shed adjoining the Marine Lake at Rhyl in the 1950s. Closed in 1970, this line was at one time the oldest 15in. gauge railway in Britain. It was an excellent example of a Greenly railway in that he designed not only the locomotives and rolling stock but also the buildings, having surveyed and planned the route in a matter of weeks. The line was a familiar sight alongside the main line from Chester to Holyhead. [E. Hughes]

The original *Little Giant*, built in 1905, stripped down for repairs by Tom Tate in 1965. It now operates on his North Eastern Railway at Haswell in County Durham. One of the characteristics of miniature steam locomotives is their longevity and that they also have a remarkable facility for going to ground for several years and then reappearing in a new guise in a new location. *Little Giant* is the classic example of this trait. [Robin Butterell]

After rebuilding, *Little Giant* was taken to the Ravenglass & Eskdale Railway to be renamed by Ernest Steel, son-in-law of Henry Greenly, in September 1965. Steel and his wife have revised many of Greenly's books and have recently written his biography. [Robin Butterell]

A comparison in scale at Ravenglass in 1965: *River Esk*, designed by Greenly, on the left; *River Irt*, rebuilt from *Muriel* as originally constructed by Sir Arthur Heywood, centre; and *Little Giant*, designed by Greenly. [Robin Butterell]

The Ravenglass & Eskdale *River Esk* passes Romney, Hythe & Dymchurch *Northern Chief* at Irton on the R & ER on 8 November 1971. Both locomotives were built over 50 years ago by Davey Paxman within two years of each other and now meet for the first time. Normally they operate over 350 miles apart. The object of the visit of *Northern Chief* was to enable the R & ER to observe the performance of a different type of locomotive while considering the design for their new engine. [George Barlow]

River Mite, the second locomotive to bear the name, is a 2-8-2 completed in 1966. It is seen here soon after leaving Ravenglass at Easter 1975.
[Robin Butterell]

The latest locomotive under construction at Ravenglass in 1974. A 2-6-2 of distinctly narrow gauge appearance, it will hardly merit the description miniature. Experience achieved with the other steam locomotives on the line, together with the benefit of the visit of *Northern Chief* in 1971, has been a useful contribution to the design. The majority of the work has been carried out at Ravenglass by the railway's own staff. [Peter Nicholson]

River Irt waits at Ravenglass, Easter 1975. The Heywood appearance of *Muriel* has been partly restored by the addition of a new cab, chimney and dome, which has improved the overall aesthetic appearance.
[Robin Butterell]

River Mite crosses the bridge at Dalegarth, the upper terminus, over Whillan Beck, a tributary of the Esk, while running round the train at Easter 1975. The three rivers, Esk, Irt and Mite, after which the locomotives are named, converge on Ravenglass to form a large natural harbour. [Robin Butterell]

Detail of *River Mite* showing the plate recording the locomotive as being the property of the R & ER Preservation Society, who raised the money for its construction. The eight-coupled wheels and chassis came from the short-lived attempt to provide a steam-driven tender for *River Esk*. Construction was by Clarkson of York with a boiler by Gower and it entered service in 1967. [Robin Butterell]

River Mite takes water at Dalegarth, Easter 1975, with the Cumbrian hills in the background. The Ravenglass & Eskdale Railway, besides being scenically one of the most attractive lines in the country, is also of particular interest to the enthusiast from an operating point of view as it has some very steep gradients in its run of just under seven miles. Several sections are round the 1 in 40 mark and near Eskdale Green there is a short length of 1 in 36. [Robin Butterell]

Overleaf: *River Mite* with a train for Dalegarth waits at Irton Road to pass *River Irt* with the Ravenglass train on 30 March 1975. [Robin Butterell]

The Bassett-Lowke 'Little Giant' *Synolda* from the Sand Hutton Railway, after running in several locations, is seen at Belle Vue, Manchester, in the 1950s, re-named *Prince Charles*. [Robin Butterell]

Later, *Prince Charles* acquired some North American appendages in an attempt to give the line a new look; thankfully, these have now been removed.

[Robin Butterell]

The extensively rebuilt Bullock pannier tank, now named *Firefly*, on the $10\frac{1}{4}$in. gauge Hastings Miniature Railway in 1966, driven by Jim Hughes, the operator of the line. Originally built in 1934, it includes cylinders from J. A. Holder's Baltic locomotive.
[Jean Nicholson]

A rarely modelled type in the larger gauges, a $10\frac{1}{4}$in. gauge Saint, *Hampton Court*, on the Hastings Miniature Railway in the 1950s. Originally built by Trevor Guest, it has been extensively reconstructed over the years.
[Robin Butterell]

The locomotives of the Romney, Hythe & Dymchurch being prepared for winter storage in September 1959. All the tenders have been uncoupled and are stored separately. This was necessary before the shed was extended to take all the engines with their tenders. [George Barlow]

A rare photograph of the three principal RH & DR types standing at Hythe in September 1959. From left to right, *Green Goddess*, English Pacific, *Samson*, one of the two Mountains, and *Winston Churchill*, North American Pacific. [George Barlow]

Constant maintenance is required on all railways whatever the gauge. Captain J. E. P. Howey watches two members of a platelaying team completing the re-sleepering of an occupational crossing near Warren Bridge on the RH & DR in September 1960. [George Barlow]

The inside of the smoke box of *Doctor Syn* in the workshops at New Romney in December 1964 showing the 24 fire tubes and four superheater flues. Apart from major overhauls and rebuilds, all repairs are carried out in the company workshops. Staff have to be prepared to be extremely versatile and turn their hand to repairs and maintenance to track and rolling stock after the running season has ended. [George Barlow]

George Barlow at the controls of a visiting Dutch-built narrow gauge type 0-4-0 at New Romney. From time to time locomotives from other lines have been brought to the RH & DR for the opportunity of running over the longest 15in. gauge railway in the world giving a non-stop run of 28 miles. [Robin Butterell]

George Barlow, Operating Manager of the RH & DR, turning the trailing coupled wheels of *Green Goddess* in the wheel lathe at New Romney in January 1960. This locomotive has been his regular mount for over 28 years. [George Barlow]

R. H. & D. R.
New Romney to
BUNGENESS
LIGHTHOUSE
Passenger Ticket Only
RETURN FARE
See conditions on back
49961

R. H. & D. R.
Hythe to
New Romney
Passenger Ticket Only
Return Fare
See Conditions on back
36521

R. H. & D. R.
Available for 2 months from day of issue
New Romney to
HYTHE
Passenger Ticket Only
Return Fare
See Conditions on back
36521

R. H. & D. R.
Available for 2 months from day of issue
HYTHE to
NEW ROMNEY
(PASSENGER TICKET ONLY)
RETURN FARE
See conditions on back
46100

R. H. & D. R.
Platform Ticket
HYTHE
1d
Available for One Hour
Conditions of Issue.
The holder of this ticket is subject to the Bye-Laws, Regulations and Conditions of the R. H. & D. Lt. Rly. Co. The Co. is not under any conditions liable for personal injury, loss, damage, delay, or detention to holder or their luggage.
This Ticket must be produced and delivered up when required and the Co. reserve the right to refuse to admit holder to their platforms or require them to leave them.
42754

Romney, Hythe & Dymchurch Railway Co.

FOOTPLATE PASS
Permit MR. ROBIN BUTTERELL
TO TRAVEL UPON ENGINE(S)
Between N/ROMNEY and HYTHE
on Engine DR. SYN working 1025 train
from N/ROMNEY on 15 SEPT. 1973
15 · 9 · 1973 Superintendent.

C 0224
R. H. & D. Rly
TRAIN TICKET
1/-
CONDITIONS
This special rate ticket is issued subject to the Regulations governing the operation of the Co. and as may be stated in their bills, Notices or Time-tables, and also to the special condition that the R. H. & D. Lt. Rly. Co. shall not be liable to the holder for any other person for injury, damage, loss or delay, however caused.

A selection of tickets from the RH & DR, including a footplate pass. On this occasion the author spent most of the day on the footplate, travelling nearly 60 miles in all.
[D. Rendell]

An interesting comparison in scale: on the left, a visiting American 'Cagney' 4-4-0, an under-scale model on 15in. gauge compared with a RH & DR locomotive, *Hercules*, built to one-third scale. [George Barlow]

Sutton Flyer from the Sutton Miniature Railway at Sutton Coldfield, which was closed in 1962, alongside *Hercules* on a visit to the RH & DR in June 1959. Note the special buffer heads to accommodate Romney rolling stock. [George Barlow]

No. 3 *Southern Maid* of the RH & DR, completed by Davey Paxman in 1927, stands alongside *Flying Scotsman* at an open day at Tyseley, the standard gauge steam centre in Birmingham, in 1973. [George Barlow]

No. 8 *Hurricane* being off-loaded at Tyseley for an Open Day in October 1974. Smaller locomotives of $7\frac{1}{4}$in. and $10\frac{1}{4}$in. gauge can be manhandled on to trailers and pulled by private cars but locomotives such as *Hurricane* require more substantial transportation. [Tony Crowhurst]

Hurricane prepares to leave Hythe in September 1973. This recent scene shows well the immaculate condition in which RH & DR locomotives are always maintained. Their mechanical state is a tribute to the devoted work of the staff over the past 48 years.
[John Preston]

Bird's eye view of *Doctor Syn* at New Romney waiting to leave for Dungeness in September 1973. The footbridge here has always been a favourite spot, not only for photographers but for observers watching the trains disappear into the twin tunnels under the road. Considerable rebuilding of New Romney station has taken place since the new company took over the railway in 1972.
[John Preston]

Locomotives *Muffin* and *Dougal* on the 15in. gauge Longleat Railway in Wiltshire on 4 July 1970. Designed by David Curwen, the 0-6-0 *Muffin* was built by Berwyn Engineering and *Dougal*, an 0-6-2T, by Severn-Lamb. Although based on imaginary prototypes, both these engines could well be described as narrow gauge in their own right. [Ivo Peters]

DOUGAL

Muffin at Longleat in November 1967, with designer David Curwen flanked by Leslie Anderson and his father, the operators of the railway at that time. [Ivo Peters]

Dougal in June 1971 at Longleat. Curwen has designed several locomotives for Severn-Lamb, but this is undoubtedly one of the most attractive small-scale locomotives ever made. [Ivo Peters]

In June 1968, *Muffin* hauls a train driven by that well-known railway personality, the Reverend Teddy Boston. Boston runs his own narrow gauge railway round his rectory at Cadeby in Northamptonshire. [Ivo Peters]

A double-headed train on the $10\frac{1}{4}$in. gauge Audley End Miniature Railway near Saffron Walden in Essex. Both locomotives were designed by Curwen, being a freelance North American type 4-4-2 and a GN Atlantic, which is here driven by the Hon. Robin Neville, the owner and operator of the railway, in the 1960's.
[Robin Butterell]

Lineside buildings were often forgotten on miniature railways so this signal box on the Audley End Railway line is particularly welcome. Most operators tend to lavish all their efforts on their locomotives and occasionally their rolling stock, forgetting that some scale-lineside accessories such as signals and gradient posts can add considerably to the overall effect of the line.
[Robin Butterell]

John Terence, of J. A. Holder's two successive railways at Broome and Keeping, running on the Stonecot Hill Railway at Carshalton in June 1959. It will be noted that, in rebuilding, the locomotive has become a 4-4-4 and has acquired a new cab. It now operates at Hayling Island.
[Peter Nicholson]

Audrey also left the Keeping Railway after J. A. Holder died and is here seen on Dudley Alexander's line in 1964. Renamed *Bubbles*, it has become a 4-6-4. The line, near Brockenhurst in the New Forest, but now closed, was operated to assist the International League for the Protection of Horses. *Bubbles* is now at Hayling Island.
[Robin Butterell]

A locomotive rarely modelled in the larger gauges is this A4 Pacific, *Sir Nigel Gresley*, a $10\frac{1}{4}$in. gauge example operating on the railway at Thoresby Hall in 1971. It was built by W. Kirkland, who also operates a $7\frac{1}{4}$in. gauge line near Ollerton. On railways such as this, with trees close to the line, leaves can be a problem in autumn as they cause slipping of the locomotives.

[Robin Butterell]

A $10\frac{1}{4}$in. gauge 4-6-0, built by Trevor Guest of Stourbridge in 1950, seen running at Lowestoft in 1964. The line is now closed and the locomotive runs on a private railway in the Midlands.
[Robin Butterell]

An early Curwen-designed locomotive in $10\frac{1}{4}$in. gauge, modelled on a LNER Pacific, runs round the lake at Carr Mill in Lancashire in August 1951. An identical locomotive ran for a time on a line at Weymouth.
[Robin Butterell]

Two locomotives of the 15in. gauge Sutton Miniature Railway at Sutton Coldfield, *Sutton Flyer* and *Sutton Belle*, on the last day the railway operated, 7 October 1962. *Sutton Belle* originally ran on a private railway near Tewkesbury, being built by Cannon Iron Foundries in 1933 from Bassett-Lowke castings. *Sutton Flyer* was completed in 1952 by T. G. Hunt of Oldbury. [Robin Butterell]

Steam-hauled until the 1960s, the Lakeside Miniature Railway at Southport was operated by two extensively rebuilt 'Little Giants', *King George* and *Princess Elizabeth*. *King George* now runs in the North of England at Whorlton Lido whilst *Princess Elizabeth* is owned by W. H. McAlpine. [Robin Butterell]

A $9\frac{1}{2}$in. gauge 2-4-2, built in the 1930s by Smith of Oldham, running on the Slate Quay at Caernarvon in June 1972. The locomotive was acquired from Captain Hewitt of Anglesey in the 1960s. Hewitt, an eccentric millionaire, owned many miniature locomotives during his life, including the present Fairbourne Railway locomotive *Katie*.

[Peter Nicholson]

A temporary line at Battersea Park in May 1972 has two $7\frac{1}{4}$in. gauge locomotives in operation. On the left, a GN Atlantic and, on the right, a NE D49 Class 4-4-0, both belonging to John Crawley.

[Peter Nicholson]

The $10\frac{1}{4}$in. gauge Poole Miniature Railway in steam-hauled days with a freelance Atlantic, *Vanguard*, built in 1948. This is now scrapped and the line operates a petrol locomotive. The Poole line is one of a trio of miniature railways operated by the same company, the others being at Bognor Regis and Southsea. That at Bognor no longer exists and the Southsea line has also abandoned steam power.
[Robin Butterell]

A freelance 4-6-4 on the Littlehampton Miniature Railway laid to the unusual gauge of $12\frac{1}{4}$in. Two locomotives were built from parts obtained from Bullock of Farnborough by Cookson, the original operator of the railway.
[Robin Butterell]

Blanche of Lancaster, a Curwen North American 4-4-2 emerging from a tunnel on the $10\frac{1}{4}$in. gauge Stapleford Park Miniature Railway, near Melton Mowbray, in September 1974. This portal of the 100-yard long tunnel is in Midland style while the other is a replica of Box Tunnel near Bath.
[G. Bell]

Line-up at the locomotive shed at Stapleford. From the left, Curwen Atlantic *John of Gaunt*, Coleby-Simkins Berkshire *Lady Margaret* and LMS *Royal Scot*, built jointly in 1970 by John Gretton, operator of the railway, and W. Whiteley. [J. Gott]

Blanche of Lancaster on the turntable at Central station with *Lady Margaret*, a 2-8-4 Berkshire built by Coleby-Simkins in 1970, in the background. North American outline models are becoming increasingly popular due to possibility of larger locomotives with the increased loading gauge. [G. Bell]

In 1973 Alan Bloom, curator and owner of the Bressingham Steam Museum in Norfolk, acquired two 15in. gauge Krupps Pacifics from Germany. Although they had not been in steam since 1953, little maintenance was required before these were running again. After re-painting they are seen here in service on the recently laid line, two miles long, at Bressingham. When the locomotives ran in Germany they carried recorders to show speed, time of journey, number of journeys and total distance covered. One locomotive has pulled 17 of the 19 bogie coaches which were acquired at the same time. These have hardwood bodies and an automatic buckeye coupling with built-in brake pipe. [Alan Taylor]

The Krupps locomotives on arrival at Bressingham just after being unloaded. They have a number of interesting features, many of them reminiscent of Greenly's work. Designed to burn coke, they work at a pressure of 200lbs. p.s.i., which is high for a miniature locomotive. The main frames are approximately $2\frac{3}{4}$in. thick and, with a full load of fuel and water, the estimated weight is $8\frac{1}{2}$ tons. Built in 1937 for the Dusseldorf Exhibition which ran from 1937 to 1939, they are named *Rosenkavalier* and *Mannetreu*. In 1949 the line was relaid in a park south of Cologne but objections to noise and smoke from local residents caused its closure.
[Michael Warren]

The Hilton Valley Railway near Bridgnorth is one of the three major $7\frac{1}{4}$in. gauge public lines in the country. Opened in 1955, it has been extended in stages until the line now gives a run of just under a mile. An automatic signal system is controlled by a staff placed over a weighted catcher when entering a section; it is seen here being deposited by the driver of A. J. Glaze's GW type 2-6-2 which is on permanent loan to the railway.
[Robin Butterell]

Daniel Lloyd, the present owner and operator of the Hilton Valley Railway, drives No. 2, *Hilton Queen*, a narrow gauge type 2-6-0. This was built in 1950 by J. N. Liversage of Herne Bay, where it operated on the pier for some time and was named *Teddy*. [Robin Butterell]

The Greywood Central Railway was an extensive private $7\frac{1}{4}$in. gauge line built by Sir John Samuel at Walton-on-Thames after the 1939/45 war. Outside the engine shed, in June 1958, are a Royal Scot and an LNER Pacific *Enterprise*. After Sir John died, the majority of the railway went to a new location near Chertsey where it now runs as the Great Cockrow Railway. [George Barlow]

A fine model of a BR Standard 'Britannia' Pacific, *Iron Duke*, on the turntable on the Greywood Central Railway in October 1954. It was built by Len Willoughby. [George Barlow]

The Great Cockrow Railway near Chertsey, successor to the Greywood Central. Open to the public on certain days during the summer, the railway has a comprehensive semaphore and colour light signalling system controlled from three boxes. Working illuminated block diagrams are used for the regulation of trains on the circuit. Here, a train drawn by a freelance 4-6-2, *Eureka*, approaches the main station, Hardwick Central. *Eureka*, one of the original locomotives on the Greywood Central Railway, distinguished itself by running sixty non-stop circuits, a distance of some $13\frac{1}{2}$ miles. Water and coal were passed to the driver as he travelled through the station to enable the run to take place. [G. M. Kichenside]

A line-up of locomotives outside the shed at Hardwick Central. As on the Greywood Central Railway, the shed is sunk into the ground, giving a more realistic appearance and enabling maintenance and steam raising to take place on elevated tracks. The locomotives are a SR S15 4-6-0, a 'Royal Scot' 4-6-0, a NER R1 4-4-0 and a Class 5 4-6-0. [G. M. Kichenside]

One of the Kitson-built Garratts of the Surrey Border & Camberley Railway eventually found its way to the $10\frac{1}{4}$in. gauge line of Sir Thomas Salt at Shillingstone in Dorset. He had it overhauled and rebuilt as a narrow gauge type and in this guise it is seen standing outside the shed in the mid-1960s. Sir Thomas built his railway originally to serve his pig farm in Dorset, emulating the ideas of Heywood on the $10\frac{1}{4}$in. gauge. Encouraged by the success of the venture, he was planning to enlarge the line, add steam motive power and open to the public but he died before his plans could be realised. The railway has recently been sold and removed. The reason for the firm of Kitson undertaking the building of $10\frac{1}{4}$in. gauge locomotives when they normally dealt in standard gauge stock was due to Kinloch, the man behind the Surrey Border and Camberley Railway, being one of their directors. [Robin Butterell]

One of the most comprehensive private railways in the country is the 9in. gauge Torry Hill Railway in Kent, the property of Robin Leigh-Pemberton. This four-cylinder *Lord Nelson* is shown being driven by its builder, J. N. Liversage. This line was constructed by the owner's father and runs through open and wooded country. Many engineering features are incorporated including cuttings, embankments, and a tunnel built on a curve so that it is impossible to see one end from the other. To add to the driver's problems, the line enters the tunnel on an up grade but leaves it falling, so it is very much a question of knowing one's road before taking over a locomotive. [George Barlow]

This scene on the Torry Hill Railway in June 1959 shows a train crossing the impressive brick viaduct. 4-4-0 *Robin*, originally an 0-4-4T, was extensively rebuilt by S. Beacon who is seen here sitting behind the driver. The original locomotive was built by B. K. Field, one time Manager of the Brighton Locomotive Works. The rebuild included parts of another Field engine of 1900. [George Barlow]

The largest model of a GW 'King' ever built, the 9in. gauge *King George V* constructed by J. N. Liversage in 1963, is shown here on the Torry Hill Railway in October 1967. Like the prototype, this is a four-cylinder locomotive. As previously mentioned, GW locomotives are rarely modelled in the larger gauges, probably due to the narrow fireboxes and difficulty of constructing taper boilers. [Terry Whawell]

Owner of the $7\frac{1}{4}$in. gauge Saltwood Miniature Railway, Alex Schwab, pulls away from the station with his GW type 2-6-0 with outside valve gear, *Maid of Kent*, in April 1960. With a chassis by Greenly, the locomotive was built by Schwab, incorporating a Goodhand boiler, in 1938. This is one of the oldest $7\frac{1}{4}$in. gauge lines still operating, dating from 1925.
[George Barlow]

David Curwen's own locomotive in $7\frac{1}{4}$in. gauge, which runs round the garden of his home near Devizes. Based on the Kerr Stuart 0-4-2ST of the Talyllyn Railway, it runs on track built of metal window section. The tunnel is of minimal dimensions and overweight drivers are liable to get wedged inside. [Ivo Peters]

This recent Curwen locomotive, built in 1973, was named after its designer by John Southern, owner of the Forest Railway at Dobwalls near Liskeard in east Cornwall. The $7\frac{1}{4}$in. gauge line, which started operation in 1969, has developed into one of the most ambitious railways of this gauge in the country. Operated by powerful North American and Colonial type locomotives with 'sit-astride' rolling stock, the line passes through deep cuttings, tunnels and over high embankments, through an area which has been planted with conifers.
[Robin Butterell]

John Southern driving *General Palmer*, modelled on a Denver & Rio Grande K36 Class 2-8-2, which came into service on the Forest Railway in 1971, designed and built by David Curwen. The Forest Railway, the Hilton Valley Railway and the Great Cockrow Railway are the most comprehensive lines in $7\frac{1}{4}$in. gauge in the country. [J. R. Besley]

A double-header with *Queen of Colorado* and *General Palmer*. The first of these virtually identical locomotives is owned by Brian Hollingsworth and runs on a recently constructed line in North Wales. [Robin Butterell]

A close up of *General Palmer* ready to leave Forest Central station. This model has completely captured the rugged power of the prototype and has converted John Southern to making the railway truly representative of the North American scene. [J. R. Besley]

GENERAL PALMER
488
RGW
K 36

The latest locomotive on the Forest Railway, a 4-8-4 of the big Union Pacific 800 Class No. 818 *Queen of Wyoming*, built by Severn-Lamb. This for an American type presents a remarkably uncluttered appearance and plainly shows the immense power available. John Southern hopes to add further locomotives in due course. [J. R. Besley]

818

The $7\frac{1}{4}$in. gauge Hilton Valley Railway celebrated its twentieth anniversary in July 1975. Locomotive No. 1, *Lorna Doone*, now 50 years old, is ready to set out from Hilton station. Built in 1925 by Lewis Shaw of Ilkeston, it ran originally at Mablethorpe and came to Hilton in 1956.

[Robin Butterell]

Several visiting locomotives came to Hilton for the anniversary celebrations. Seen here is *Zebedelia*, based on a Mozambique narrow-gauge engine designed and built by Roger Marsh, being driven by its owner, Ken Blackham.
[Robin Butterell]

Another visitor was 0-4-0ST *Kanchenjunga*, being a model of an engine of the Darjeeling Railway owned by Brian Hollingsworth and built by Coleby-Simkins. Waiting at Stratford Brook station, it is driven by John Harrison, one-time driver on the Fairbourne Railway and now stationmaster at Tan-y-bwlch on the Festiniog Railway. [Robin Butterell]

On show at Hilton was the $10\frac{1}{4}$in. gauge model of a 2ft. 6 in. gauge Leek & Manifold tank engine owned by Brian Nicholson. Built by Coleby-Simkins, it is hoped to run it on a new line near the site of the original Leek & Manifold Railway. [Robin Butterell]

The recently completed 4-8-2 + 2-8-4, *Kilimanjaro*, is a model of an East African Railways metre gauge oil-fired Garratt. Both the prototype and this model can claim to be the most powerful locomotives in the world on their respective gauges. Measuring 19ft. 6in. over couplers, it has four $3\frac{3}{4}$in. × $5\frac{1}{2}$in. cylinders, a 17in. diameter boiler and water capacity of 50 gallons. Fired by domestic central heating oil, it operates at a pressure of 115/120lbs. p.s.i. Neil Simkins of Coleby-Simkins, the builders, is seen on the right. Here the locomotive is preparing to leave Stratford Brook station on the Hilton Valley Railway. On a test run, over 100 passengers were carried, using only half-power. Owned by Brian Hollingsworth, it should have ample opportunity to show its potential on the 1 in 22 gradients on his own railway. [Robin Butterell]

The Hilton Valley Railway's latest locomotive, a 2-8-0 built by A. J. Glaze, modelled on a prototype running on the metre-gauge Antofagasta-Bolivia Railway in South America. Named after Daniel Lloyd's father, *Michael Charles Lloyd MBE*, it was to enter service soon after being on static display on 19 July 1975. [Robin Butterell]

Romney, Hythe & Dymchurch Railway locomotive *Winston Churchill* working a train from Hythe on 28 August 1973. This photograph was taken during a two week period of running experimental trains at a later hour than normal.
[Tony Crowhurst]

All photographers who have contributed material of their own or from their collections are thanked for their assistance. In particular, I would like to mention George Barlow of the RH & DR for help and advice, R. H. Fuller of Bassett-Lowke for the loan of photographs from their collection, J. T. Holder for a selection of photographs from those taken by his father, the late J. A. Holder, and Douglas Ferreira for the use of photographs from the Mary Fair collection.